Forgiveness
Mary P. McAllister

STUDIO GRIFFIN
A Publishing Company
www.studiogriffin.net

For information, contact:
Studio Griffin
A Publishing Company
studiogriffin@outlook.com
www.studiogriffin.net

Cover Design by Ruth E. Griffin
Image by © paul /Adobe

First Edition

ISBN-13: 978-1-954818-56-9

Library of Congress Control Number: 2025904306

1 2 3 4 5 6 7 8 9 10

CONTENTS

PREFACE

Writing this book was a very special experience for me. It flowed from a place of freedom and healing that I can only credit to my time and relationship with God. I shared a portion of my story in my first book, Salvaged: From Damage to Destiny. In that book, I shared how hard it was to bounce back from the breakup of my marriage of 33 years. I also shared a few of my experiences of the painful moments that took place away from the eyes of others. Those experiences held me hostage in my feelings and emotions for quite some time.

There is no way to capture the fullness of what goes on behind the scenes in a troubled marriage. In my Salvaged book, I only shared the moments that I felt were most relatable. But a troubled marriage can affect the heart and mind when the vows which both parties took, under the oath of God and man, are broken. For thirty years of marriage, I lived under the assumption and belief that my marriage was going to last forever. It never entered my mind that it would be any other way.

The vows I made to my husband on our wedding day were very personal to me. Even in my wildest dreams, I never imagined my situation would change so drastically. From being married, to being divorced and single again. From nurturing and supporting our family in the home, to having to rebuild my life, career and finances outside of the home. Everything about my life changed in the most unexpected way and I felt so unprepared for my new life after marriage. No one prepared me for the drastic changes that divorce brings. Yet these changes are happening far more often in marriages than many would think.

I wrote this book to share the other side of my story. Not just the overcoming side where I overcame my own emotions, and negative thinking about my marriage and the effect its ending had on my life. But in this book, I wanted to share the side we rarely hear what it feels like to truly forgive. Forgiveness is a step further than overcoming. Being able to be in the same room as someone is not the same as forgiving. I found so much healing in forgiveness. It allowed me to look for ways to go on and find the peace I needed in order to live a successful and productive life. In doing so, I first had to be freed from all malice and ill feelings. If you are at a similar place in your journey, I hope this book will aid you in also taking the freedom leap that will move you past overcoming into forgiveness.

INTRODUCTION

While going through my transition from being married, to being divorced, I needed to let go of some feelings of resentment and animosity. I felt betrayed and pushed out of the life I had known for so many years. I felt cheated of my happiness and my happily ever after. I was hurt. A part of me wanted to hold on to my anger, hurt and frustrations that allowed me to keep holding onto a grudge. That was what my natural man was telling me to do. But my spirit man was telling me to forgive and allow healing to be a part of my testimony.

In my journey to forgive my husband, I realized how many parts of me were still holding onto every emotion that prevented me from walking in forgiveness and healing. Forgiveness starts with a heart to forgive. A heart to forgive will aid you in extending forgiveness even when you feel it isn't deserved. These next pages are the extension of my testimony of how I got over my emotions of "what was" to become a healed overcomer. And how I moved forward in forgiveness and made the devil mad.

AGAINST THE ODDS

Infidelity, to me, is the most hurtful of all of the many reasons for a marriage breaking up. The act of infidelity is very painful but is still something that can be forgiven. I have heard from and know of many spouses that could not or would not forgive the infidelity that destroyed their marriages. When infidelity enters a marriage, the trust that was once there is completely destroyed and is not easily rebuilt. However, if a couple wants their marriage to be saved, it can be saved. In order for that to happen, they both have to be on the same page. They both have to agree to save the marriage. Otherwise, it can be a waste of their time.

The infidelity can be forgiven, the couple can pick up the pieces of their marriage and continue with their lives. By keeping the lines of communication open on both ends (which is a must), the process of reinstating the trust that was lost can begin. All of this is possible when you have the help of God working on your behalf. There are some things we just can't do without the power of God working in our lives. Those who do not have that relationship with God, often have a harder time getting beyond the infidelity that happens in their marriage.

Certain couples can't get past the hurt and betrayal because they are trying to do it by their own power. You by yourself are powerless without the power (help) of God. A marriage can only be rectified if both parties want it to be. No one person can make a marriage work successfully. Both parties have to be willing to agree and forgive in order to rebuild what was broken. It is a losing battle when only one person is fighting the war.

God will only do what you will allow him to do, but you must do your part and put in the work. Even though my marriage ended in divorce, I was able to forgive him. I was successfully able to live my life. Through God's complete healing, I also lived in peace and harmony with my ex-husband. I wanted the marriage to work but he did not, so we ended our marriage. I had to deal with the pain and disappointment but, with the help of God, I was able to forgive and be okay with time.

You have the power to forgive within you. I know that it is hard for you to believe this when you've been hurt so badly. Trust me, I know. However, it is not impossible. The God we serve has given us the power to do all things.

> *"If thou canst believe, all things are possible to him that believeth".*
> *Mark 9:23 (KJV)*

You have to make up in your mind that you will not carry the heavy burden and weight of holding onto unforgiveness, pain and anger that come from you being hurt. You have to be willing to let it go and free yourself. As long as you are carrying all that anger, you are only hurting and harming yourself. While you are nursing your bitterness, the other party is going on with their lives. They are not wasting their time or energy being upset with you or crying because things went sour. This was definitely the case in my situation.

My husband never missed a beat with continuing to live his life while I was yet nursing my wounds. You will never know the joy and peace you so deserve, until you let it all go. You have to really fight the enemy for that piece of your mind. Satan does not want you to be free. He also does not want you to be happy. He does not want you to know the joy of releasing all of the weight of the hurt, anger, stress, and embarrassments. Satan definitely does not want you to release all of the other negative things that are sucking the life out of you because of bitterness. You deserve to be happy and free... so go for it.

LETTING GO

When we are doing things on our own, and not seeking the guidance and direction of God, we will make all kinds of bad decisions. We will look at our lives, the things from our past that have inflicted pain on us and get fixated on the negative alone. It is hard to look beyond that and see anything better for us. Believe me, there is so much more ahead of us that is better for us. God's abundant blessings are not cut off from us, when we go through the valleys of life and get lost in the wilderness, those same abundant blessings are still there waiting for us to take possession of them. But we must be in the right standing with God to receive them.

You can't access the full blessings of God, if you are not pure in your heart. You must release any malice, hatred and evil you hold in your heart for anyone. All of that is like toxins in your body. Anything that is toxic cannot render anything good for your life. Toxic thinking is not good for your mind, body or spirit. It can prevent you from functioning as you should, because you are having to deal with those feelings of animosity and resentment towards one or more of God's people. I say God's people because we are all His children. He created us all.

We have to become little children (childlike) again. Children will fuss and fight, but minutes later it is as though they never fought or were mad with each other. We, as adults, feel like we have to hold on to stuff, or be mad and angry until Jesus comes. You do not have to hold on to those toxic feelings. You can let it go and forgive. I am not saying that you should become best friends or buddies, but you can live peacefully even with those who have inflicted some kind of pain upon you. The word says in Romans 12:18 KJV "If it be possible, as much as lieth in you, live peacefully with all men". That includes those who have wronged you.

What if God never showed mercy and compassion to us every time we hurt or disappointed him? What if he never forgave us for the many times we said or did something that was contrary to his teachings and the guidelines laid out for us to live by in the His word? God gives us brand new grace and mercies every day. We are not by any means worthy of them. How can we not forgive our brothers and sisters and expect God to forgive us over and over again?

Who are we that we feel like we have the right to hold on to our anger and frustrations with someone? Who are we that we feel like we have the right to continue asking God to forgive us for that hateful thought, or that ugly act we did to someone? The word teaches us to do unto others as we would have them do unto us.

Colossians 3:13 says, *"Bear with each other and forgive one another if any of you has a grievance against someone."* (NIV) Forgive as the Lord forgave you.

One of the greatest challenges I ever had in my life, as a teenager, was learning how to forgive others. Someone whom I was close to, did something to me and I felt it was unforgiveable. I held on to a hatred like none I'd ever known in my life. The very sight of this person made my blood boil, and it was not a good feeling. Yet, I was so bent on keeping my hatred and contempt for the person that those toxic feelings stayed with me for years. Throughout that time of my blood boiling emotions towards that person, I was still going to church and singing in the choir like the righteous Christian I was portrayed to be. I was being hypocritical, and I was only deceiving myself, which I figured out later.

I thought I was teaching this person a lesson, but she was enjoying her life whether I was in it or not. I was the only one on the outside being miserable and unhappy over something that was detrimental to me. She did not do anything so vile or dire to me that would have caused me to die from what I felt was done to me. But I was still always mad for no reason and not nice when I should have been. My toxic feelings and reactions to her went on for so long, that I got to the point that I didn't quite know how to get beyond what I was dealing with... hatred.

I wanted to forgive and be free, but I didn't know how to do what needed to be done to truly forgive. You can hold on to the bitterness so long that it becomes a part of you and much harder to release. Finally, I decided that I was tired of carrying hate towards another person and sought the Lord to help me get over my disappointments and emotions. One day I came to myself. I opened my eyes and my heart to allow the love of God to penetrate and replace that ugly place of hatred with the beauty of his love. I was completely freed of that awful weight. There was no fun in it, and I was the only one miserable. I finally forgave and it was so refreshing to be able to breathe without the strain of hate gripping my heart. It was liberating! I had overcome my first real bout with hating and learning to forgive.

Matthew 6:14-15 says: *"For if you forgive other people when they sin against you, your heavenly Father will also forgive you. But if you do not forgive others of their sins, your Father will not forgive your sins."* (NIV) We sin every day in some way: a slip of the tongue, a careless and thoughtless act, a thought we should not have had, or by so many other sinful acts we may commit. God does not hold these things against us. When He is within His right to do so because we are found guilty, He still does not. So, who are we that we think we have the right to hold on to stuff others do to us and not have a forgiving heart?

I was determined after that awful period in my life that I would never allow hate to take a seat in my heart. Hate moved in and tried to make a home with all intentions of staying there forever. Forever meant that hate planned to go with me to my grave. If hate stays with you, all through your entire life, it means you have no intentions of seeing Jesus in heaven. Hatred of any kind is not allowed in heaven. I never want to not have control of my emotions to that degree again. I thought I would never be able to release that stronghold of hate from my life. God is so good that He will free us from the bondage of hate when we ask and allow Him.

Not forgiving someone does nothing to the person you are hating, but it will do a lot of damage to you. First, it will rob you of your peace of mind and it will add a level of stress to your life. It will take a bite out of your overall character. Not forgiving can negatively distort the personality of a humble and loving person who people love and enjoy being around. The favor of God and man on your life will be blocked by what hate has caused you to become because you would not let it go.

FORGIVING ALL

There were some events that took place in my life, which left me so damaged and hurt, until I thought that I could never forgive. In my first book, Salvaged: From Damaged to Destiny, the incidents I shared for the average person would have been unforgivable. But, in my experience, there is nothing you can go through in this life that God can't put behind you in order to bring the spirit of forgiveness into your life. For you, it may be hard to believe that you can endure so much hurt and pain (especially from someone you love) and still forgive them and live in peace and harmony with them. But with God everything is possible. I am a living witness to every word written in this book.

> "But Jesus beheld them, and said unto them, With men this is impossible; but with God all things are possible." Matthew 19:26 (KJV)

The Bible says, with God all things are possible. If you want it bad enough, really believe in the power of God. You will see Him move in your life and remove all the bitterness. I know what the power of God will do if you allow it to work on your behalf. When you have the love of Christ in your life, you know how to love as Christ loves. You can love past the hurt and hate you may be experiencing. Actually, your love will eradicate the hate. Don't you know that love is more powerful than hate! Some of the things we do hurt our savior over and over again and he still loves us. So, who are we not to forgive others?

It is so important and necessary that we have a relationship with Christ. When we are faced with certain situations in our lives that we have no control over, we will have an advocate who will step in and give us all we need to become overcomers. When we have done all that we know to do, God will step in and finish the process which will lead to our victory over that particular situation. We have a tendency to forget that it is God who is the source of our very being and not us. Our very existence is because of the grace and mercy of a loving and caring God. God wakes us up every morning and starts our human engine to get through another day.

God gives us the strength we need to endure until we get to the victory.

We lack the gratitude and appreciation for all that we are blessed to have in our lives. We take this precious and beautiful existence that we have been given for granted. Do not assume we are so deserving that God is obligated to grant us a new day. God is not obligated to do anything for us. He does it because He loves us, and He is a merciful God. God gives us new mercies every day from the moment He touches us to wake us up to grant us another day. We did not earn a new day by any great thing we did in the previous day. Yet, He allowed us to see another day anyway.

There should not be a day that goes by where we fail to give God thanks for just waking us up in the morning. We could have laid down to sleep and not opened our eyes to see a new day. But God allows us to see another day over and over again. Throughout the course of each day there are so many things we may say or do that disqualify us from being worthy of getting the blessings that we continue to receive from God daily. We may have spoken harshly or offensively to someone who did not deserve it, or we may have had an impure thought that would not have pleased God. But He did not hold it against us.

God loves us in spite of ourselves. I believe that there is a way to say anything and not be cruel or offensive to anyone. God does not keep his blessings from us just because we are so undeserving. He shows us grace and mercy daily. We are not perfect beings, but we should strive daily to be the best we can and apply the word of God to our life so we can continue to grow in grace.

WHAT WAS LEFT OUT

No one has the discussion regarding divorce before marriage. That is simply because we never enter a marriage with the intent to get a divorced later down the road. The goal is to stay married until death departs us. Well, that was not the case for me but nevertheless, that is not something any couple has in their mind when they decide to take the vow of marriage to each other. There are counseling sessions before you say 'I Do' to help you prepare for your life together and hopefully for a lifetime of happiness. I can assume the discussion of divorce is never brought up. This is not something anyone ever wants to discuss in pre-martial counseling. No one wants to fall in love with any intentions of spending the rest of their lives with, then start off talking about a plan of divorce, just in case the marriage fails.

When a marriage goes south, the end result is a divorce, you are totally lost and without any direction on what, where or how to navigate your life. You gave your future to someone whom you thought was going to stick with you through the thick and the thin, in sickness and in health, for better or worse until death do you part. When one spouse decides it is too much, that is when you find yourself at divorce court ending a marriage. It is not something you made plans for, or had any kind of guideline to tell you how you are to cope with the situation you are now facing. In so many cases it's not just you, but there may or may not be children involved. The big question, hovering over your head, is 'What Do I Do Now'? As painful as it is, you know that you have to try to pull yourself together, begin to make plans to begin again. Such a bummer! This is not what anyone had planned for their future.

Divorce is so unfortunate, marriage is a godly plan, it can be so beautiful. Even with the ups and downs, it is still the best way, it is what God ordained for us. In my case, I loved being married, the good outweighed the bad. I admit there were many hurdles we had to overcome, many times we wanted to quit but we did not quit. First of all because we loved each other, secondly, God was there giving us his divine guidance. God did not fail us, we failed us.

When you take God out of the equation (marriage), you begin to think, I can handle certain things on my own, that's where you make a grave mistake. A marriage is not made solid the day after the honeymoon. It takes a lot of time, patience, compromise, getting to know and understanding each other. There are so many other things that you have not learned about each other. You cannot possibly know a person or understand a person, until after the marriage and you have lived with them for a period of time.

Dating only gives you a glimpse of whom a person is and what they are all about. It may take a few years before the two of you are truly in sync with each other's moods, way and vibes. You need to begin, to adjust to certain facts, you are no longer in your own personal world or doing things your way. That was fine when it was just you, but it is no longer you, it is now us. The word "Us" means, we have to compromise and amend the way we do certain things. You not only have to think for yourself, you have to now think for your spouse. It is really truly an adjustment, but if you stick with it, you can have a wonderful life with the love of your life.

Having someone in your life to love and who loves you is a great feeling to have. However, having someone in your life who loves you like the Lord loves you is so much better. The Bible says in 2 Corinthians 6:14, *"Be ye not unequally yoked together with unbelievers."* (KJV) In other words, when you both are headed in the same direction, with the same intent, it makes the journey so much easier and better. When you and your soulmate love the Lord, you can love each other with an assurance, no matter what the two of you encounter, in your future, God will get you through it all. There will be absolutely nothing, that the two of you cannot overcome when you walk with God. God knows that the enemy hates the institution of marriage, he wants it to always fail, but God will cover those who live for him and love him. Don't you know, God is love! He loves us even when we don't deserve to be loved.

We are imperfect creatures, flawed, and fall so short of God's glory, but God still loves us. Is that not the kind of love we want to experience with someone during out lifetime? Don't we all want to experience joy, peace, happiness, and the excitement of sharing this life with someone special from day to day and year to year? The marriage vows are sacred and so wonderful. It was very special on the day you said, 'I Do', and it can be that way till death do you part.

EYES WIDE OPEN

When things start going south, you may see signs of the changes happening in your marriage. Your spouse will send out signals to let you know, they are not happy in the relationship for whatever their reasons. You can address this, or you can try to let it ride itself out. It's so much better to address it, try to figure out what is happening and what went wrong. Honest communication with each other will open doors for discussions of the what, why, when and how things went wrong. It will be uncomfortable but is extremely necessary. You may not get the result you want, but you will get some clarity.

You begin to question whether or not you are doing something wrong: Was there something you did or did not do? or Is there someone else in the picture? These are things you need to know. If your spouse indicates to you that they no longer want you, believe them and start making decisions concerning yourself. It will be difficult for you to believe how someone who claimed to love you so much can now tell you that they don't love or want you anymore. It happens!

You cannot make someone love you and want to be with you if they don't want to be with you. No matter how much you love them or can't imagine your life without them, it is not going to work unless both of you want the same thing without reservations and with a true commitment to each other. There can't be a third party connected to your life if you are going to save your marriage. Life is too short to waste your precious time trying to convince someone, who has already stressed to you they no longer want to be with you, to love you or stay with you. You have to value yourself even if you are not valued by anyone else. Do not settle for someone else's crumbs when you know that you deserve a whole meal.

Just face the facts, sometimes certain things do not last, and things do fall apart. Well, that may be the way it turns out, but that is not the end of the story or your life. Sure, you are at that crossroads of divorce, but it can turn around and lead you to the best life you've ever imagined. Divorce may cause a lot of things to happen and change in you, but it does not kill you. You are still alive, ready to live, and start the next chapters of your life. A part of that new beginning is learning to forgive.

You went into the marriage with high hopes, but you were not prepared for what you now have to face. You are now divorced and have to try to put the pieces of your life back together. There are so many questions. The first one is how am I going to get through this catastrophe? The entire demise of a marriage is catastrophic. Especially to the one who does not want a divorce. It can be devastating if you are not strong in your faith. Having a God centered life, and a strong faith will help you tremendously when you get to that stage. You can maintain your focus to some degree but seek your heavenly father to give you strength to do what you must do now. Know and believe that this is going to be the beginning of a new life for you.

You will be fearful that you cannot do this thing called life by yourself, because you have been sharing life with someone else for a while. Let me tell you, God will show you where your strengths come from and just how strong you really are. You have no idea just how strong you are until you are faced with the hard things in life. God has given you power, which you have never tapped into, and when you need it the most it will kick in just like superpowers. Just like the fantasy superpowers of your favorite DC Comic or Marvel character kicks in when there is a need; your strength will amp up inside of you. You will be amazed at how strong you truly are when you have to make tough decisions about where to begin again and how to recover. You will realize that you have not tested your faith as you should have, and you will start to put it in fifth gear in order to make all kinds of new moves for your life. Although you may be unable to see where your life is headed, your inner strength will keep you moving and give you the faith to roll with the punches.

You now know that you have got to make a plan and work that plan in order to secure a future for yourself. You may have to relocate, change jobs, go back to school, etc., but whatever you do, know it is going to be a faith move. You did not have a course beforehand, on how to survive a divorce. There was no handbook given out on what to do in the event the marriage ends. All you have now is you, your faith, and a God who loves you still. Remember that you are a smart, intelligent and capable person who has the ability to be anything you want to be. At this point that is like money in the bank. If you believe in your heart and know that God's got you, you are better off than you can imagine.

NO TIME TO WASTE

While you are going through, waiting and hoping by some miracle your marriage can be saved, do not lose yourself completely or become a doormat. Especially when you are no longer treated like the wife of a loving and caring husband, but just another person of no significant value by someone you have vowed to love and care for until death do you part. All of the things happening in your life at that time seem so obvious. Something is wrong in your marriage, and for reasons you may or may not understand, you are a victim of unwarranted abuse; be it physical or verbal. This can diminish you to a level you do not deserve. You can end up getting the leftovers of attention, care and love from your spouse and will make yourself be okay with the insignificant amount of love they now choose to give to you. That is not okay! It is not acceptable, and you do deserve so much more.

Sadly, I wasted ten years waiting and hoping he would notice I loved him so much and so hard. I did not want to let my marriage go so easily and so willingly. I would allow myself to spend my weekends with him where I was given a false sense of hope. That was my bad choice and my mistake. I waited a long time, just to still end up with the short end of the stick in the end. I did not pay attention to the verbal and nonverbal signs he was giving me which said, 'I don't want to be your husband anymore.' His actions said, "I have found someone I want more than you." I ignored all of the signs by choice. I'd say to whomever this applies, do not waste so many years in denial. When time has passed and those years of you waiting are gone, you will have aged and still be all alone. Your spouse has moved on and uses you when he or she feels like it. You are too valuable, and your happiness matters as much as theirs. If you cannot be valued as yourself with them, then maybe you will with someone else. Make room for someone new by letting the excess baggage go. Free yourself and find yourself again. Again, your happiness may just simply be being free to be by yourself, to enjoy doing just what pleases you and doing some of the things you gave up in order to share your life and time with someone else. I have realized time for myself has been refreshing and totally liberating. I call all the shots now since I am single and that has not been the case since I was nineteen years old. That is when I got married, at the early age of nineteen. I do not like the idea of divorce, but unfortunately it still happens. Life does not stop because of divorce. Only the way you live it changes. You are the one who will control all of the vehicles now, you are the captain of your destiny.

TASTE THE JOY

There is a special kind of peace and joy that comes with knowing that you have released all of the bad feelings and have completely forgiven someone for the hurt they've caused you. I remember the moment I said I forgive you. It allowed me to release all of those frustrations of hurt and anger. I was in church, and the preacher was teaching on forgiveness. Can I tell you, that word hit me so hard! I began to meditate on the sermon of forgiveness. As I thought about it and meditated on it with my spiritual mind, I was able to release all of the anger, contempt and malice I was holding against my former husband... and it felt oh so good. I felt like I released so much pressure, that was so heavy. And the moment I released it, my body went limp like letting air out of a balloon.

Carrying around those things in your heart are not just heavy for your mind but can also affect your health. Those tight muscles are filled with stress sometimes because you are holding on to stuff you need to release. Your spirit man can't grow, you need to be willing to make room for that growth, by letting some things go. Let it go, so you can go on with your life. Apply Ephesians 4:31-32, *"Let all bitterness, and wrath, and anger, and clamor, and evil speaking, be put away from you, with all malice; And be ye kind one to another, tenderhearted, forgiving one another, even as God for Christ's sake hath forgiven you."* (KJV) You will be glad you did. The weight of all you were carrying will be lifted off you and you will be free. Give it all to God.

Sometimes we get hung up on how much we were hurt, and we want to hold onto the pain so tightly that we cannot begin to think rationally. We become obsessed with the idea that vengeance is our best gratifier. We want to use whatever means we have access to in order to get back at the one who hurt us. Hear me now: that is not the best way to go.

First of all, if you are professing to be a child of God, and you are living a godly life for him, you must not choose this route. God has given you everything you need to get through this rough passage in your life. So many people want to use their children to get back at their ex-husbands. That is wrong and the thought should be cast out at the beginning of the inception in your mind. I do understand that when you are hurting and want to feel some vindication, you will do just about anything. It is a natural response but that does not make it okay to go in that direction. The children had nothing to do with what has happened to you and your spouse. They are innocent victims and should never be used as a pawn in your desire to get even. I remember going through all of those thoughts and emotions. I had to endure through the rough passages leading up to my divorce as well as the aftermath of the divorce. As I was going through everything, I was always concerned about how my kids were being affected by all of the drama and unhappiness going on around them.

Because of my Christian walk, love for God, and my faith; I never tried to use them in any way to make myself feel better by hurting him. I made it a point to make sure they knew that their father loved them, and that he was dealing with some things in his life that I could not explain. I never bashed him, nor did I talk negatively about him around the children. At the end of the day, he was still their father and had been a very good father. It was not my job to get revenge for what he did to me and the family. Romans 12:19 says, *"Do not take revenge, my dear friends, but leave room for God's wrath, for it is written: "It's mine to avenge, I will repay," says the Lord."* (NIV)

The children knew a man who showed them love throughout the years, it was not my job to taint what they knew to be good and real to them. Even when I was not yet at the place to forgive him, I kept a cordial relationship with him just so I could keep them uplifted and not unintentionally cause them to interject hostility towards their dad. Some might say, "You cannot have that kind of strength to maintain that kind of relationship with someone who has done all those hurtful things to you and still concern yourself with how they feel." Well, I did it! It wasn't easy, but I knew it was not impossible. God will show you just who he is even in what looks like your darkest hour. The strength you get from keeping the lifeline to Christ open in your situation will propel you to your victory through the situation and lead you to your win.

IT'S YOUR TIME

You may have to start the forgiving process by first forgiving yourself. So many of us will start re-accessing everything that happened and start pointing fingers at ourselves. We want to accept blame for things we had no control over in the first place. We start telling ourselves, maybe if I would have done this or that maybe we would not have been divorced. Beating yourself up over something you could not control does not change the situation.

In this process, you must get to a place where you accept things for what they are. Please forgive yourself for thinking you could change the mindset of a person who changed their mind about how they felt about you. Once someone decides they no longer want to be with you, there is absolutely nothing you can do about how they feel towards you. Stop beating yourself up, you could not prevent the end result from happening to your marriage or relationship. When you know that you have done all you could do and nothing you did changed the situation, just accept it for what it is and make your next move for you.

Start redirecting the love you have for them to yourself. Start loving on yourself and appreciating the beautiful and wonderful person God created you to be. Even when no one else loves you, love yourself. Start putting the time and energy you tried to give your relationship all those years into you. You will never regret it, and you will see that there is so much more to you than you thought. Pick up those dreams and visions you put on hold for the sake of being with someone else.

There is still so much more in you to be birthed. This could be the opportune time to start letting your creative juices flow through you. Abandon all animosity, anger, frustration and the negative things which held you hostage for so long. You are free to forgive all and start to live your life to the fullest as a totally new person. There is nothing wrong with starting over. Sometimes you have no other choice but to start over; and that in itself can be the beginning of the best chapter of your life.

You have to be really tired and fed up with the weighted unhealthy situation you are dealing with to free yourself for something better. I heard someone say, "In order to have something different, you have to do something different." You cannot keep doing and accepting the same old things. You should expect to see or get something different. You have to make some changes to the way you do things. Start by forgiving and move to the next step. Get yourself a plan and start working it in order to have a better life for you.

Fear wants you to think that you are not capable of branching out and taking your life back. Do not allow fear to stop you, greater is he that is in you than he that is in the world. 2 Timothy 1:7 says, *"God hath not given you the spirit of fear; but of power, and of love, and of a sound mind."* (NIV) Keep your mind made up. You are going to start a new and wonderful life which you so deserve. You have given, sacrificed and did all you could to make the marriage work. You have exhausted all of your physical, mental and spiritual resources. Now it's your time to move on and make a fresh start for yourself. Go and let God do the leading all the way. Seek His direction in every decision you are making. He will not lead you in the wrong way.

KNOWING WHAT'S VALUABLE

Life is so precious and uncertain, you have to learn to value every moment, second, minute, and hour of every day. Life is to be lived to the fullest by purposefully doing what is important and meaningful. You cannot waste any of the time you are given in life. Once it is gone you cannot go back and retrieve any of it. Many times, we take things for granted by living carefree and frivolously with no regard to what the consequences may be for us. We live like we are entitled, and that God is obligated to grant us everything we think we want without the need for us to be grateful for everything He has already given to us.

The fact God woke you up to see another day is nothing but the grace which we were not entitled to receive from Him. God is merciful because He loves us so much. He grants us daily mercies and extends grace over and over again for each precious day that we have been graced to live. What will you do with your precious days? Who will you help throughout your precious days? How will you spend your precious days? Or will you utilize your precious time and days to belittle, abuse, hurt, offend or destroy someone else? We have to be mindful of how we use all of our time from day to day. You only get to live this life once. It's worth it for you to make it the best life ever. There are many things that can be replaced in your life, but you only get one life. Do not get hung up on the many possessions you have, that you fail to value the time and the people you with which you are already connected.

So many people are caught up in material and tangible things they acquire. They make the mistake of putting the most value on those things and become very slack in the attention they give to what is most important, the people in their lives. We have to be able to appreciate the ones we claim to love and show the abundance of that love to them, and not to our possessions (cars, houses, clothes, etc.). Possessions are things that can be replaced if something happens, and you lose all of it. Your life and the people in it cannot be replaced.

The people and relationships you have in your life are hard to replace once they are lost or destroyed. Those relationships are priceless and should be treated as such. Value the ones you love. Avoid placing them below or beneath the possessions you have acquired. If God blesses you to have those things, then life happens to take them away by some unforeseen circumstances, know he is still the same God today that He was on the day He blessed you with the things you lost. God will restore unto you everything you lost. There is nothing too hard for God! He will always stand by his word.

> "But my God shall supply all of your need according to his riches in glory by Christ Jesus." Philippians 4:19 (KJV)

God will restore back to you everything you lost and more. Keep in mind that what you have acquired in life is by the grace of God. The fact He blessed you with the tools and resources to obtain them, should make you thank God. Never assume you did this all by yourself. Without God, there is no you. Know that if He did it before, He can do it again.

LOVE TO LOVE

We were taught that a family that prays together stays together. I believe that to be true. However, this only works if the husband and the wife are committed to God and the word being applied to their household. It is hard to get the same positive effect of staying together through prayer if the house is at any time divided.

> *"And if a house be divided against itself, that house cannot stand."*
> *Mark 3:25 (KJV)*

The marriage will not work if only one spouse is praying and seeking God's guidance. If husband and wife are not working as a unit to keep the family together, eventually the whole thing will fall apart.

A mother can be all she can to her children, but she can never be the father they will need. The same is true for a father. He can never be the mother those children will need. Not even in giving all that he or she has and being the best parent he or she can be. This is not to say that one parent can't be a great parent on their own, it only means they can't be both the father and the mother. They can be either a great mom or a great dad.

Even when prayer is not done as a family unit, it still does work. So never cease to pray even if you have to be the only one praying. God will honor and answer your prayers even if they are yours alone. When things do not work out the way you want, keep on praying. God knows what is best for you, He will answer according to what is best for you and your family.

Love people the way you want to be loved. God shows us how to love, unconditionally. We must learn to love genuinely. I grew up in a household where even though we knew we were loved; we never expressed that love verbally. We never questioned if we were loved nor did we ever doubt that we were loved, it was just understood. The way we were cared and provided for showed us that we were loved. We would always spend family time together and enjoyed each other as a family. Many years down the road, when I was married and had a family of my own, I learned the importance of saying

I love you. I made it a priority to express love verbally and with hugs and kisses. My kids were smothered with all of that kind of love. I never knew what I'd been missing until then. Although this did not diminish the love I grew up with, it was still a good and loving life. I just never remembered hearing the words I love you in our household.

Nowadays, we are more expressive and affectionate than when I was growing up. Touch is so important; people feel loved and cared for when they are embraced. I personally am a hugger. I love people, I always want them to feel the love which we all crave. You cannot expect someone to show you love when you are always a grouch. If you never smile, never be friendly, you shortchange yourself, and people will avoid being around you. A warm smile will generally get you a warm smile. It takes so little to smile at someone.

It's okay to love on the ones you love and show love to people you care about. God loves everyone. We are given daily examples by our loving and caring God. Let us not fail to show love to those who struggle with how to express how they are feeling. Some people find it harder to step out of what they have known most of their lives. Let them see in you the affectionate one they have never seen or known. They have to be shown how to be affectionate by those who experience love in that way on a daily basis. Then by allowing themselves to become a loving and caring person.

When genuine love and affection is expressed by sincere people it will be felt in a positive way. People will know when you are real and when you are fake. They are given instincts by God. You can feel genuineness when you encounter it from someone. You can sense when something is not quite right. God has given us everything we need to recognize truth and sincerity. John 8:32 says; *"And you shall know the truth; and the truth shall make you free."* (NIV) Just because we were not exposed to certain wonderful things in life, as we were growing up, does not mean that we are exempt from having and experiencing them. Learn to love to the fullest and walk in all of the love and beauty of God's wonderful blessings. Know for yourself the wonders of life that are available to you.

You may ask, how can I know? There is this wonderful book of truths that will show and tell you everything you need to know, and it is called The Bible. Start reading and studying the word of God regularly to find the answers to the mysteries of certain things you have not been privy to in your earlier years. God's word will bring clarity to the things you may question and open up a new understanding for your life.

I'm sure many of you were brought up in church, attended Sunday School and were taught many Bible stories but never taught how those stories were related or would relate to you and your future. Those were good and intriguing stories for young minds (and still are for children today) because they kicked our imaginations into gear. As we got older and began to understand our surroundings better, we needed a bit more clarity. We are not the originators of the events we face from day to day. These life problems and situations we deal with today are the same that were experienced in the events of the Bible. We were being prepared in our early church upbringing through those stories to make us ready to deal with them today.

The world and the times have changed, but life and its ups and downs remain the same. We are equipped to handle and deal with life's ups and downs in different ways, but we are getting the same results as they did in Biblical times. We receive the same grace and mercies God shows to those we read about in the Bible stories we were taught in Sunday school. God has not now, nor will He ever change. His love and blessings remain the same and always will.

Growing up in Sunday school most of us were taught a simple song that said, 'Jesus loves me this I know, For the Bible tells me so, Little ones to Him belong; They are weak, but He is strong. Yes, Jesus loves me, Yes Jesus loves me, Yes Jesus loves me, For the Bible tells me so'. This song was drilled into us when we were children, and it is still relevant today. God never stopped loving us no matter how disobedient we were or how many times he had to forgive us. He always receives us back into His arms as His own.

RIGHT CHOICES

I have learned that everything I do in life begins by me making a decision. In other words, if I just react and make a decision without even giving it a thought; sometimes it may be the right decision and sometimes it may be the wrong decision. I have realized that I need to stop and think before I make any decision. We are tasked every day to make many choices about our lives. Even choosing to forgive or to hold a grudge is a choice made by a decision and conscious effort.

For me, I wanted to hold a grudge, but I just could not do it. I knew it would put too much pressure on my spirit man. That meant, I would be filling my life with hate and all of the attributes that accompany hatred. I wanted to just stay mad and be mad because I had the choice to do so. But if I had gone down that path, before I realized it, I would have become a bitter and unhappy person. I knew I wanted my life to be better than that. I wanted to be happy. So many people think It's easy to be mad and mean, but it takes a lot of effort to hold on to those heavy feelings that weigh heavy on your heart and your mind.

The best thing to do is release all of those ill feelings and allow yourself to be free. Whether your marriage is saved or not, you owe it to yourself to let yourself be happy. The decision release those heavy emotions is in your control and only you can choose to release them. It takes a strong and determined person to get past all of the hurt and pain they have experienced in order to forgive and even to go on with their lives. Forgiveness is a form of freedom. It takes away the tug on your heart. You already know it is wrong; it releases the pressure on your mind to retain the reasons you chose to not forgive.

In your mind you replay the events that caused your anger. Replaying those events will keep everything at the forefront of your mind so you can continue to dwell on it and therefore making it even easier to stay in that bitter state. You can choose to break free from that mind set. Even with this in mind, you have to pull from the strength you get from God and your faith so you can see and reach those better days ahead. It is definitely a process, like anything else, but there is victory afterwards.

Life is meant to be lived. If you are stuck in one state of mind, you are not living your life. It all goes back to the choices you make about your life. Do you want to be happy, or do you want to be bitter and angry for the rest of your life? Do you want to feel joy and peace, or do you just want to be miserable and left alone? The joy of the Lord is there for you if you want it.

God has so much more that he wants to give us and do through us, so we have to continue to fight to be our best. We have to fight to be able to be worthy vessels of God who are able to respond to His call to be used by Him. No matter what we have been through, God desires for us to help enlighten others around us about what He can do for His people. When you have been beaten and broken so badly but you have beaten the odds, you have a testimony you can share to share with others about the great and mighty God we serve.

We did not make the survival list all by ourselves, we have the grace of God giving us strength and directions as we make wise choices and decisions about our next move. We had someone in our corner, who was praying for us and interceding on our behalf as well. We all have angels watching over us and interceding to the Father on our behalf, be it a family member, friend or spiritual leader.

We cannot allow our disappointments to keep us from being and becoming vessels used by God to help someone else. What you went through is not unique for you alone, so many others have suffered and gone through some of the same things. They are trying to figure out how to get their life back. They are lost, confused, and still trying to figure out how they got to this point in their lives. Some are still looking for the answers on how and why, and are accepting shame, guilt or blame on themselves in areas they were not to blame. Many people are in need of hope and help. Those who have survived should be willing to help and share their testimony of how they made it through. We have stories, but who is willing to be transparent enough to share and help someone else? Who can break away from the shame and fear of what people will say and think about them in order to be a blessing to another person? Who will make the decision that will help another make that initial step towards their freedom from the past that has held them hostage for so long?

You can be the change for someone who is dealing and trying to get out of the rut they have been locked in for so long. You can be the one who administers hope to the one who has lost all hope. You can be the one who will help the person blinded by deceit and misuse to be able to believe in something that is bigger than us.

If you are one who has not been able to let go of the past and forgive those who have wronged you, I encourage you to take this moment and let it go. It is not worth it for you to be miserable, mad and sad because you were hurt or disappointed by someone. It is time for you to take back by force what the devil stole from you, which is "YOU"! Make a decision right now that you are going to begin to live a happy and prosperous life in Christ Jesus. As you go with Christ, you will start to reap all the benefits God has for your life.

TRANSPARENCY

At this point, I want to share with you my personal knowledge of knowing how hard it was to move on and to get to the place of forgiveness. When I made my initial move to reclaiming myself, it was so very hard in the beginning. For the first six months, I was not able to sleep in the bed by myself. I had been married for so long, until it was impossible to sleep without that warm body next to me. I think what was the hardest part about the whole thing; knowing that this was now my new normal. There was no man to come home to and prepare a meal for or share details about our days. That was probably the hardest part about my initial move.

Nonetheless, I was able to get past that and really find me. The nights were long, but they were also quiet. No one there to argue with, question, or become wrapped in my emotions. There was not an opportunity to want to ask questions why or do any probing about anyone or anything. I no longer had to endure the verbal abuse which was just as bad as a slap in the face. It was just a perfect time for me to focus on me and work on my plan for my future. At the time, I was not sure of what was actually going to happen, but I learned to appreciate that time later down the road. Let me tell you, there is nothing in your life you face that God won't get you through. After all of this, I was able to forgive and move on. God is so faithful, and He helps us do the very things we consider to be the unthinkable.

I encourage you to forgive whomever for whatever and you will never regret it. The peace you will have will be priceless. Love yourself like you love others. You're worth it! You have given and given to others and so many times you have been left with the short end of the stick. So now is the time for you to allow yourself the freedom to get it all back. Be the person you always wanted to be. Go to places you planned to visit. Live in the freedom of finally releasing everything in forgiveness for them and for you.

ACKNOWLEDGE-MENTS

Special thank you to Jarrell J. Kirk for assisting with her administrative skills and support, and to Erica S. Johnson for always being there with her professionalism, support and encouraging me to write another part of my truth.

A very special thank you to Ruth Griffin for adding the finishing elements to getting 'Forgiveness' to print. Thank you, Ruth!

ABOUT THE AUTHOR

Mary P. McAllister is the author of 'Salvaged-From Damage to Destiny,' which is about her divorce and survival afterwards.

Mary spends quality time with her family as she enjoys the benefits of holding on to the faith that got her through a very crucial and tough time in her life. Life is good and God is good!

www.ingramcontent.com/pod-product-compliance
Lightning Source LLC
Chambersburg PA
CBHW061719120626
46550CB00003B/1287